My Own Sanity

By

Amy L. Phillips

ISBN: 1-4107-3208-8 (e-book)
ISBN: 1-4107-3209-6 (Paperback)

Library of Congress Control Number: 2003091533

This book is printed on acid free paper.

Printed in the United States of America
Bloomington, IN

1st Books - rev. 03/06/03

"You save yourself or you remain unsaved."
Alice Sebold

<u>Lucky</u>

Acknowledgements

I want to thank everyone who helped me help myself, those people who have always been by my side. Those deeply loved people are: Alan C. Phillips (1948 – 1998), Christine L. Attaway, Charles and Magdalen Phillips, Dana Baenen, and
Billy S. Stevens. These are the people who provided me with both stability and understanding. You have all taught me how kind people can be and what a gift life truly is.
Thank you also to all those friends that helped in their own way:
Christopher Garza, Melissa Garza, Crystal Lewallen, Amy Pike, and the Parkers.
Thank you to John Attaway for giving my mother a second chance at happiness.

Table of Contents

Acknowledgements v

Preface xi

Mission 1

Gifts 2

Motivate Me 3

Classical 4

Veterans 5

Search for Self Love.. 6

Time Away... 7

Alaska... 8

Sparrow 10

Refresh 11

Mothers 12

Mothers & Daughters.. 13

Grandmother.. 14

Grandfather.. 15

Jamie 16

Molly 17

Kiss of Love 18

When You Leave... 20

I Love You 21

Marriage 22

A Drop of Love... 23

The Bay 25

Hearing Things 26

You are My Love 27

Everlasting 29

Free My Mind 30

Confusion 31

Succubus 32

A Creeping Sensation 34

My Box 35

Cuban Funeral 36

Winter Comes 38

Survival 39

Earth Demon 40

Erosion 41

Lethargy 42

Wise One 45

Devil's Blanket 46

That Night 48

Envy 50

Serpent 51

Go Away 52

Attrition 53

When Love Leaves 54

Away 55

I Smoke to You 56

Wrong Love 59

Grabbing Tree.. 60

Games are for Fools 61

I Don't Believe in You 62

My Harbor... 64

Little Girls 65

Please... 66

Relationship Blooms 67

Daddy's Pride.. 69

The Day He Strayed... 70

Father Left Me Twice 71

To Dana... 72

Missing You 73

Goodbye Father 74

The Ring 75

Alone 76

Cage... 77

Endless 78

Fear 79

Awaiting Therapy 80

Panic.. 82

Dreams 83

Insomnia 84

Fear of Sunlight... 85

A Good Day 86

A Thin Line 87

Today 89

Waiting 91

Upstairs Neighbors 92

Black 93

Selfish 94

Broken Wall 95

Don't Look 96

Waiting for Death 97

Dead Room, Dead House 98

Death Comes Quickly 99

Rain 100

Number Four 101

See 102

Yarn 103

Locked In 104

End 105

Mr. Elephant & Mr. Rooster 106

Good Morning Prozac 107

Preface

The following poems are a collection that began roughly 7 years ago. During that time, I have dealt with my own personal demons and life's hardships. Being faced with chronic depression, panic disorder, and obsessive compulsive disorder, I learned to relieve my stressors by the way of writing. I wrote during both the ups and the downs. Sometimes things made sense, and sometimes things did not. Be it manic or depressive state, I tried to use my writing outlet to record my thoughts. Writing in turn, soon became my best therapy. It has helped me to deal with the death of my father, self medicating through substance abuse, and an abusive relationship.

There is really no order in which these poems are listed. They vary from manic to depressive and panic phases. I hope by reading these poems, you will gather a better understanding of what it is to feel so imperfect in such an imperfect world, the tricks the mind can play on the body, and the terrible fear that can encompass ones life.

Mission

Give me the strength to walk alone
To follow my own convictions
To cast my insecurities aside
Not to be fooled by others
Nor weak in the presence of fear
Guide me toward prosperity
And lead failure astray
Knowledge shall send me to wisdom
To clarify and purify my soul
Allow my eyes to see beyond
And relish in the beauty of nature
To walk ahead of the others
Driven forcefully by destiny and fate
Do not allow melancholia to arise
And let my gait command respect
Give me the ability to step back
And see each moment for what it is
Let truth be shown in many hues
And simplicity be my goal
Striving constantly to better my being
And never to look back at regret
I alone rule my domain
And set forth to conquer all

Gifts

Let me taste life's gifts
To dance naked in the sun
Drinking from earth's pure water
Splashing against the stones
Reaping the fruits of our fathers
Fresh juice to feed my soul
Giving me life
Feasting on nature's materials
Cherishing all it sends forth
What comes from its soil
To learn from the bush doctor
Found in St. Lucia
To be cleansed by nature
Freeing myself with its herbs
With its roots
And travel to Souifere
To see the floating markets
Their small handmade rafts
Gently keeping the water below
Living off their sales
Of conch and coconuts
Let me taste life's gifts

Motivate Me

I think you want me to appreciate your grand beauty
And hold it in my hand
All comes from one
One greatness
I feel the stone's energy flowing through me
My entire body sweats
Yet my eyes and nose chill
To be alone with my thoughts
And inspiration is what I need
To make my mind not blank
And I want to feel love one true time
With such intensity my life depends on it
With such purity my health thrives on it

Classical

The notes flow casually through the air
I become listless
Caught in a trance by the melody
Each cord massages my mind
And takes me to a place of peace
Air around me becomes a soft pillow
Becomes a warm embrace
Anxieties drift away with each stanza
This timeless music has soothes many hearts
Its beauty has been known for centuries
Our common bond
The notes that save the soul

Veterans

You lie beyond the willow tree
Under years of earth
Daily people pass
Children play
Life's circles continue
Not paying you any mind
At your height we all were proud
Now you are a mere memory

Three days a year
Your fellow men honor you
They are what keep you alive
As generations pass, their numbers grow lower
Forgive us for our stray
Forever your life is our history

You lie beyond the willow tree
And one day you will be part of it
Shall we realize and give you praise
You, a victory of man

Search for Self Love

As I sit among the burning candles
Their flicker the only light I have
I know serenity
And the simplicity of beauty
Each of the three flames dancing in shadows
Cleansing my skin with sunflower oil
To wash the impurities away
And I try to make myself aware of my surroundings
Every shape, every scent
The way the hues play off each other
I want to taste the pleasures
To explore imagination
To not feel regret
And to find a knowledge foreign to me
What is my reason for being
To feel at ease and love myself

Time Away

I make mistakes every day
Daily another mark goes up
I often wonder if you are a mark
If you are an err in my life
All are consequences I have to face
I cannot tell you which is worse
A mistake of your love
Or without your possible love
Maybe what I need is time
Time for self-exploration
To look deeper inside myself
To absorb my surroundings
To soak in the beauty
And to realize the beauty within myself

Alaska

I want to live in Alaska
The sun never to set in the summer
And never to rise in winter
I want to see the independent gold miners
To see the moose and elk
And to live a life of simplicity
To be a disciple of Walden
I want to live at one with nature
Not to feel nature pushed aside

I want to feel free
And start over
To live among the adventurers
Not to be antisocial
But rather to find my inner peace
To focus on myself
To create a better me

A me not afraid of others
Not always fighting my nerves
I want to sit outside
And soak in life
Absorb the beauty found on earth
And search for the true meaning
The truth found within myself

To leave everyone behind
To leave the human routine
And to live off our natural resources
And raw materials
To use the earth as it was intended
To eat, breathe, and live the earth

I want to learn what nature has to teach
And to learn it unselfishly
To learn to trust
And believe in my own convictions
To be able to express myself
Openly and honestly

I want to know my life has reason
That I have a greater purpose
Not to serve and be true to others
But to serve and be true to myself
I want to live on a higher level
I want to love what I become

I want to live in Alaska

Sparrow

He lands in the tree
A constant curious attitude
His sinewy feet proudly perch
A noise out of range
Causes flight
His small wings spread
A gentle breeze is created
We seldom notice their bodies
We seldom listen to their song
Such precious little creatures

She stopped on day
And looked to the sparrow
And she saw his beauty for what it was
And for a moment
Time stood still

Refresh

Revitalize me
Take these weary thoughts
Make them true
Chang my soul
Uncallous me
Softer petals must be grown
Wash away the fear
Ease my known
Begin the saving

Amy L. Phillips

Mothers

Her soft touch reassures
All is true
An understanding unknown to others
But known to us
Continually redeveloping, maturing
Partly because of you we reach near perfection
Yearning for that glassy coat
You make me human

Mothers & Daughters

The grilled cheese sandwich I made
Wasn't the same
As my mom's were
It was my medication when ill
My fire when cold
My joke when sad
My hug when lonely
My challenge when bored

It was the quiet, simple way
Of saying everything to me
Alone now
I make my own sandwich
Which is not a tunnel of awakenings
But just a sandwich

Grandmother

With strength every morning she rises
To live another day
Moving with pain
Keep inside to show yourself strong
Some days bring sadness
Part of your routine
Without power to do your own
A butterfly in a net
One day the sun arose with you
A smile spread your face
And the days became warm
Bleeding hearts bloomed on the bush
Squirrels came to see
For years all was good
Then frost grew
The bush's blooming ceased
And you had to put your child down
When will your bleeding hearts bloom again?

Grandfather

How can I express
What a man should be
Kind, strong, understanding, faithful
Full of love for his family
The essence of truth

There is one man that I know
That fills all of this
And I am proud to have his
Blood in me

Jamie

On the floor she sleeps
Close to my side
Never mocking, never taunting
Always feeling love
Her brown eyes gaze for the simple
Entranced at life
But not asking much
Needing only food and love
She strives to please
Never judging
Courage and loyalty is all she knows
Her perfect soul
From which we should follow
Put our differences aside
The simple animal can teach us much

Molly

Molly Tater Lightning Bulldog
Molly Sue Sweet Tater
The best puppy in the world
Half blue heeler, half bulldog
White with scattered brown freckles
Ears big enough to fly
She smiles when she looks at you
Loves everyone she meets
Tail wagging a million miles an hour
Jumping in circles
Chasing her tail
Leaping up from the ground
To lick my face
I always know she will be happy to see me
No matter what kind of day I had
No matter what I look or feel like

17

Kiss of Love

I want the love
That with one kiss
Should last all eternity
To take my breath
From deep within
And rise above all else
To carry me about
And never to fray
Nor tear from rough winds
This love born from Heaven
Its grip forever tight
Purity which comes
In no spoken word
But feel of floating bliss

Oh to find such a kiss
A search that leads travels
To world's end
But a search none the less
Of which one must embark
Driven by desire alone
To feel the rain dance
Upon one's lips
And rose petals
To caress one's body

Oh to find such a kiss

When You Leave

And I shall love you forever
You hold a place in my heart
Deep inside me you shall endure
Thriving upon my all
So dear to me you have grown
Should the day come when you leave
Close to me you will remain
Living each moment with me
And I shall love you forever

To always gaze into your eyes
And feel your warm touch about me
Your full vision shown in my dreams
Your laughter echoes in my ears
I am overcome with love
And I shall love you forever

To feel your comfort at just that moment
When I yearn for a warm embrace
Your love which makes me human
And taught me to love again
I shall never forget you
For you are my comparison for all others
And I shall love you forever

I Love You

You enter my thoughts
More often now than ever
I try to imagine that perfect thing
When those words will pass your lips
And the way I am overcome
My breath stolen for a moment
Only to return at a quickened pace
And I hope you always remain
As you always are
That strength I rely upon
When those words pass your lips
My love for you will be renewed
And I will remember what brought
Me to this point
And there it will stay
Bound tight to my soul
You are that something
That I have longed for
And through it all
You lead me back
To myself
For in myself
I feel your every part

Marriage

Walk with me
Through circles I know
And take my hand
Expose your will
Cover yourself with the fruits
Search for your other
And do not be afraid to fall
Your wings will carry you
To understanding
Seal your strength
Forget your vice
For love is truth
We must see ourselves through clearness
Disregarding shallow layers
Uncover the soul
Spill your joy into generations
Do not fear hardships
Bravery shall shine through
Replace misconception
The gate will open
The souls will become one
Forever bound eternally

A Drop of Love

You, my everything
My day, my night
My eyes are lost in you
My heart caresses you
Thoughts of reason long gone
And we jump with closed fists
Reaching
Tortured by your words
Misplaced in memories
Searching for grand riches
Sensation, awareness
And the sky mocks me
Heavyheartedness suffocated me
And there I sit
And it is quiet
Yet I stay
Forced to cling
Suggestively grinning
Color me with your magic
Cautiously awaiting love's rush
Please overcome me
Still we exist helping each other
Challenge me
I am willing to climb the mountain
Willing to look over the edge
And I believe my wants are too much

23

Through closed eyes, I see you – a drop falls
I know that I have been touched
One true time
If never again, at least once
Part of something I will never lose
And for that I am grateful
To know you, to love an angel
And for that I am grateful

The Bay

Follow me down to the bay
To walk with me along the pier
On a bench we enjoy each other
The wind is warm and comforting
You look so beautiful
Watching how that water moves
The waxing moon hangs overhead
Your presence makes me feel safe
My worries are gone
My fears floating away with each ripple
As I look at you
That is the only place I want to be
My love for you is vast
Like the bay
Always changing, but never fading
And you will always be a part of me
Forever to be my one true love

Hearing Things

Last night I thought I heard you say you loved me
Why is this something I can never be sure I heard
Is it that I want to hear it so desperately
That those three words can mean so much
I would feel so close to you
Or did you really say it
Did it accidentally slip out
I hope the second is the case
Our life together would only get better
And how far could it go from there
A new level of our love would be in our mists
So I will keep pretending I heard you correctly
And someday perhaps I will hear you correctly

You are My Love

I want to take you with me
On a new journey of new places
To a foreign land of riches
Where together we can enjoy the splendor of life

Hand in hand along our travels
Feeling the earth beneath our feet
Fresh lilac lingering in the breeze
And we stop and gaze in amazement

Let me cast a mold of you
So I can remember your every perfection
And sing to me all your frustrations
And I shall cast your tune to sea

My untold love will show through my acts
And my lips shall dance upon your body
Your arms tightly gripping me
Pulling me close as if I were your clothes

Together we lay
Dancing with one another
Tingling with blissful sensations
United as one our souls collide

I have found peace in you

My strongest emotions ever
Your eyes keep me still
And together we remain

My love is raised to new heights
And I am aware of every part of you

Everlasting

How can one word
Spoken in your voice
Bring about such great
Change in me
No matter how bad
I may feel
One sound
Can enlighten me
To life my spirits

Even though I know our
River is dry
Your power fills my heart
I sit and wonder
If all this will ever fade
You will always hold
It is what you do with it
That will determine my fate

Free My Mind

How can one describe a feeling
Nothing, numb, insensate
Inanimate, repose
Free, unconscious, calm
In a state of dreaming
Does your mind free itself
If you do not allow it to be freed
If you are so afraid and lost
Does it pass you over
Place you somewhere else
Allow your subconscious to
State itself without your fears
Holding it down
Or will fate take hold
And let things occur

Confusion

The love hate animal wheelchair
Culture through mirrors
I toss the fish into the solid oil garden
And it catches me – il mal occhio
And I shake its scaly cockroach paw
It frightens me and I run into the desert
To free myself
From hates beautiful armchair
The capitol tastes me
Long luxurious high heels
And of perfect red and tiger paws
Ice freezes and makes me bleed
I find a soul on the under shoe
Stick it on the doll
My arms are tied with ropes of rain
And I look at you and laugh
Until water comes
I feel the sun dried cherries
Drip down my spine

Succubus

Her eyes are dark and blank
Red stockings cover her legs
Black lace wraps her breasts
Her craving sends her to the night
Fat pouting lips slowly parting
She is an orchid
A minion of the evil empire
The last of the wild offspring

She looks at the paintings of babies
How perfect and exotic
Painted in a row
On coffee colored stain

Snow falls steadily
Smoke rises from the earth
With every step she takes
Winter air is biting

She sees him sitting against a doorway
He is low on the human food chain
Dirt embedded under his nails
Soot about his cheeks
No one will miss this one
He can bring ecstasy to her dead veins
Restlessness is too hard to hold back

He looks up to her shocking beauty
She oozes sensuality
From every pore on her body
One can taste the lusciousness with ones eyes
Her breasts swell with every breath

She sinks her teeth into his neck

He is paralyzed by the sybaritic grandeur
Of her body, her great beauty
She sucks his being
His body tenses in rapture
Yet he keeps quiet until death comes
She lets him fall to the street
Wipes the blood from her chin
Done feeding for the night

A Creeping Sensation

Invisible bugs crawling o my skin
Adrenalin Rushing through my veins
Though I am sitting still
I can see my arms shaking
Head feels light and airy
Throat void of saliva
Eyes darting up and down
Nerves firing out of control
Cold hands and feet

My Box

Don't disturb me when I am in my box
The door is locked
Shades are drawn
In the corner of my box
Wrapped in blankets
I sit and cry
My eyes throb with pressure
I have been here so long
All I know is a heavy heart

Please don't try to break in
I will be crushed by the pressure change
I would let you in if I could
But my legs cannot walk
My voice is gone
Please just leave
Walk away and don't look back
I am too afraid of myself

Cuban Funeral

Not to see what seeing has to see
Blind visions of solid mops
Restless in the air
Balloons caress inner babies
Monkey in fame
Fortitude war edition
Materialism recoil shank
Distrusting length
Dripping decipher
Omnipotent

Rogue
Steep fistulous harem
Kudu freely run headless
Seven knotted knives
Autocrats fearing life
Glowing golden leaves peel
Slaves to bond
Feeling is stripped out
Left to die

Emotional uproar release
Loss of words to tie tongue
Truth spills out red
Twisting and taunting dagger
Passion is out of him

Demonic fret love not
Heart numbs
Water of drink

Idolizing wrongly disillusionment
Wonder will retrieve revive
What left but pain to over
Sink not to die
Grab the book of life
Truth comes out in misunderstood words
By whom
Too much time

Focus on not delay
Caution us in time of surrender
Lust over
Dread attachment of heart
Red
Oozing from traveled feelings
Within proportions tied uneasily

Coils, circles played all
Plagued all
Dissatisfaction of what known flier
Handle too smoothly
Expect to see through stains
Army of true territories
Surging forward to battle

Avoid enlist present
Funeral of guilt
Penitent
Violent arcane men

Winter Comes

The geese in the field
Tell me that winter is near
They crowd our town
As do seagulls in the summer
Their voyage to warmth is long
I know soon they will be back
And the apple tree will grow full
The bees will again buzz

Until then I sit and wait
Wrapped tight in my blankets
My teeth grabbing for each other

Survival

Survival of the fittest it what we are taught
Do not cry or show a sign of weakness
Weak will perish, strong will survive
And so on, and so on, and so on
Keep fighting, pushing the weak ones down
You will receive the great reward
Make the weak live together
Let them fight one another
To see who is the strongest of the weak
Let that winner come to us
So we can show him his is still weak
And we keep fighting one another
And so on, and so on, and so on
Until there are only two left
Both believe themselves the strongest
Yet neither want to risk death
They come together
Realize the wrongs they have committed
But it is too late
They have ruined mankind

Earth Demon

Willy what have you done
Stolen an angel from our mists
So young and gentle
Fair Amanda
So many spirits you have broken

Society tries to understand your state
You, tortured by your own demons
Are you aware of the evil you have done
Now your life is in God's hands

For hers, a life cut short
A father's dreams destroyed
His beautiful daughter never to age
Never to marry or bear children

And for what
Why must we destroy each other
May God have mercy on your soul

Erosion

See the mighty wall crumble to sea
Can you hear the ancient
Calling loudly to us all
We can reach out and touch gods
Our burning, yearning arms
All lost, left alone
Fear of mountains higher
Sun burns to flakes
Path an art booming blunt
And I see your demons
Starting, piercing, cutting, stabbing, drowning

Lethargy

I don't like done what I see
Jungle I hear does man
Eight dancing women
Journey institutions general
Repeated on calloused high
Realize in him people tenant
Monster character
Stops
Hiding mules backward
Cities are flooded younger
On, ability transmission cerebrum
Immovable south, log back
Extraordinary haunt inexpensive
Produce studies sybarites
Unstressed

Courage rebate walks
Nemea where once lived
Rotting defiance
Sew into twists white lisle
Parturition our world disgrace flesh
Eating our windows
Filling our churches, schools, streets
Clay museums, banks of gold
Bargained love lost but mother
Eyes paper birds speak

Various governments exhibit obligations
Mobs sensation
1996 running crimes illustrate
Admiration suffering
I asked

Which revenge went depressed
Conscious laughing eyes
The irritating girl
Conflicts doted
Respected six needles
Mere everything in reach
Holds years house disturbing
Roving beside
Lighting tree scene
Company evidence
Imperishable rebellion
Office descending
Panic necessary

Standard of faithful arms
Coaxed red lines
Blue with inferiority
Tails of incorporated seals
Sturdy pulsating
Falling night drops
Flowing, floating
Dance of mystery
Ghosts parade on floor area
Two rows – red on blue

Twelve ideas left to spill
Blunt cuddle bones
Dripping yellow marrow
Terror-stricken reams
Clouds break to liquid
Balloons drop
Cliffs of steep

Amy L. Phillips

Broken pain shatters
Lifeless screams of hurt
Can I hurt you more
None left to chase

Wise One

I know you want to make me better
But who is to say that I am worth it
This rush of information overwhelms me
The more you want, the less I do
Your whole truth revolves around paranoia
The final separation and leading away
I worry that you know what I am thinking
That you want to take charge of my soul
Just close my eyes, cover my ears
Hold my breath and don't let me think
How can I begin to object
You're right, I am wrong
Don't trust the government, trust us
Don't trust the church, trust us
Give your life to us
For only we can save you

Devil's Blanket

Their worth is not knowing of what shall come
My heart weeps for you
My arms scream for you
Your heart yearns
Your eyes burn
For I have to power to create
I do not see, hear, feel, touch
Heart is closed
Souls can see
What I answered
Your eyes pierced me
His glances ravished me
A frightening feeling
Your eyes burn me with scornful notions
Gold and temperate voice
Soft whispers
Sharp words
Heart is full of life
Stricken by love
Nothing more than a multi colored quilt
Waiting to wrap around you
My eyes sweat with intensity
Cannot run
Paralyzed by curiosity
Your porcelain hands are cold
Sending shivers to me

A loose unwanted quiver
You hear the faint words of wisdom
And finally I am free
Save this cold and demented world
It will taunt and mock you
And I alone lay on the burning ground
My hands begin to blister
Body dripping from perspiration
All is silent
Laying for an eternity
But then I see him again
With wings and voice spread
Walking toward me
I see him again
Angry eyes slanted
Stone heart pounding
Throbbing head
Huge violent flames
Unbearable
Frightening vision
Feared by all
The devil himself
Wondering where the children may be

That Night

She puts the deposit in the back room
Turns out the lights and flips the sign to closed
She locks the front door of the bar
The cold night pushes her quickly to her car
"Excuse me"
Startled she turns
"I have been watching you work all night"
Closer he moves
She can smell the alcohol on his breath
"You are so beautiful"
She turns and opens the car door
His hand grabs her arm
"Don't you like a compliment?"
Fright begins to creep up
He leans in close to her hair, runs his finger through it
"You smell so sweet"
She screams and struggles
No one is around to help
The lot is empty and the night is dark
He pushes her into the car
Slams her head against the dash
Blood rushes from above her right eye
"Shhh, I am not going to hurt you"
Forcing the driver's seat to recline
He pushes her back
She struggles to get him off of her

"Shut up! Stop making it worse"
Her body tenses as he kisses her neck
She is still screaming
He slaps her across the face
And presses his manly hand over her mouth
With great rage he pulls up her skirt and tears her underpants
Her mind begins to run
Wondering if this is really happening

He forces himself inside her
As a tear falls from her eye
The salty tear mixes with the blood
She feels her body tearing
The pain is so intense
She numbs herself focusing on the dome light
Her leg scrapes against the emergency brake
With her mouth covered
She can smell the cigarettes on his hand
Taste the sweat on his palm
As quickly as it began, it ends
In a final deadening thrust
From the depths of hell
A moan escapes his contorted face
Her body is shaking uncontrollably
He slaps her again
Punches her in the face
He zips his pants and raises off her
He leaves the car
Walks into the night and out of view
She lies there in shock and disbelief
She is not aware of the tears
Not of the pain he left behind

Envy

I push you down
Relate it to me in words I know
You look at me with green sights
Plant your trees in Center Square
Sprout to miles
Do you see my sight
Color my dreams
Behold the dawn
Your words are cleverly twisted
But I see your lines
Expose you green lines
Expose your green motives

Serpent

You speak to me like snakes
Your tongue twisting
Words of roses at hand
Swirling behind me
Ago paths crossed in super excellence
But left with jinx
Such is friendship when eyes don't meet
Or views stray
The river divides
And farther apart we grow

Go Away

Why do you steal my trust
Everything you say is reverse
A backward walking stick
Pouncing on me
Like a cat with a toy
You lost me long ago
You still impose
You've exploited my wisdom
Turned my ideas back
Through a two-way mirror I view you

So don't pull me close again
Nor will I ask this of you
I've gone farther
And you will stay behind

Attrition

Why do you always bring such pain to my heart
Your words come cold to me
Your kindness spins like a top
I begin to wonder if all you've said is truth
Your motions confuse me
I thought I could trust you with my feelings
I thought I could open to you
That I could love you freely
My return request was simple and pure
Your heart in return
Yet you are unable to show your love to me
My ideals of you and I are no more
Pleasure that came from thoughts of our future
Left me
I know things are different now
With every word that leaves your lips
So please don't expect me to be the same
Nor ever feel the same
My heart has begun to fall from your grasp
And I don't know if my mind will allow
You to regain it
You brought me to a feast
Yet you did not let me eat
And daily my heart grows thinner

When Love Leaves

Today I heard your voice
And no emotions arose
Our conversations empty
The silence between us unbearable
I feel sorry for you
What made you the way you are
Why won't you let me show you the higher road
Do you ever feel alone
Do you ever wish I was there
I know you do
Without your words
Do not tell me your evils
We cannot continue like this
Only our fears keep us together

Away

Do you want to taste my
My flesh
You are a murderer and thrive on my life
I see your death in my own eyes
I can taste your horror
And you give me power
Do not think that I am here to give you satisfaction
Believe that you are here to feed me
So do not rape me anymore

I Smoke to You

I am afflicted by trepidation
Are you an imposture
Always being elusive
But I am the only one inside me
To hear my inner most
Your knowledge cannot reach me
And I smoke to you
So don't take me gently
I know you can't
How I want
You look pale against the backdrop
Cold, black eyes
But you won't let me in
Why don't you speak to me
Your anger carries you
I can't imagine your frustration
Nor why you take it out on me
Do you try to make me feel like this
A manipulative trick
It angers me that it seems to work
I didn't think I was so weak
But you play on my addictions
And you know how to make me disordered
You terrorize me
My soul
You force me to believe you

That your breath is all I need
To give me life
Pulling me together
Not letting anything be unleashed
Does it excite you to scare me
To make my heart race
Just hold me close
The way I need you to
How I remember it was
Just laying next to you
And I don't understand
Are you really that cunning
You feed me sorrow
Reminding me of who I am
You are magnanimous
The courageous one
You bring me paranoia
I just want you to pay attention to me
The safe, wanted attention
Don't give me your tendencies
For there are two types of relationships
Direct and inverse
And where do we fall
I pray we can move beyond
And come together once again
But I still feel
The invisible bugs crawling about my skin
It all feels so real
And still I wait to hear from you

Why do I make you so important
Putting you up so high
I wander through life
An eccentric zombie
Having everything, knowing nothing
You need to live
You are a vampire
Who needs to prey on me

But do you understand
You don't know the true me
A neglected plant
Needing only your compassion
I want you to be consumed by me
My fairy tale has not begun
That is what I strive for
That perfection
Of what I aspire to have
The growth of us
To gain the nurturing
That we both need
But how long will we remain

Wrong Love

As I sit and wait, my mind begins to wander
Am I ever going to be all you need
My boredom is overbearing
I remember how we use to love
That wasn't true love
You have just fed me lies
They have rolled off your tongue
I am not the only one you think of
The wrong love

Grabbing Tree

You remind me of a dark night
Able to hid things
Behind the wicked tree
Whose branches curl and twist
Stars provide little light
To see portions of you
Only what you want seen
No matter how much I want
Or try
I cannot take you all in
I should be afraid of you
But your branches attack me

Games are for Fools

No longer will I play your foolish games
Be second to anyone else
What your reasons may be
I cannot continue much longer
I have wrestled long enough with that notion
And I deserve more
Your priorities deceive me
I need to be your first
If I leave, do not follow
I will be too far-gone
Moving ahead and beyond
I won't have time to search for you again
And you will have lost me
I cannot express this to you now
Figure it out on your own
I will be waiting silently
Make your move
I shall analyze you from afar
Currently at your side I wait
Wondering what you will do
You must determine if I am worth a sacrifice

I Don't Believe in You

I don't think you realize how much pain you actually bring to me
It may come as sharp words or sharp actions
That cut deep into my soul
Your purpose behind all of this is by far unknown to me
And I only see confusion lying ahead
At times I feel you truth is shown
But to what extent
Your tendencies are to draw me near then force me back
Speaking devilish words that linger in my brain
And they forever peak through my happiness
No matter where my heart may be
My revenge to you will someday come sweet
And cause you pain
To try to teach you your wrongs of man
But you won't expect it
And it will be my present to you

I am not here to give you sanctuary
Nor to relieve you from your sorrows
You have managed to tear down parts of me
But now I am able to look at you through a new set of eyes
Never to be blinded nor ever blink again
For every day I shall remember your errs
And place them in a secure place
That only I can reach
That only I can understand

In fact you think you know me
My thoughts, feelings
But be aware that I hide from you behind a solid mask
That you forced me to construct
And now my goals are different
My thinking shadowed by a cloud of hate
Marked by your ideals

Someday I will see you again
And I will laugh and spit in your face
I will rip out whatever I have left in you
And set it afire
And smile at the dancing flames
Your screams I will not hear
Nor care of what pain you suffer

My Harbor

All I really want
Is to feel that yearning
That true love
When I enjoy the moment
Yet can't wait for the next
And always longing for the previous
The constant of passion of lust
The stability of certainty
To put my all at ease
To fall in love and have it returned
To fall in love with falling in love
To be touched by the warmth of a heart
Of purity and honesty
To be safe and secure
In unconditional love

Little Girls

We need to make sure
That our little girls know
They aren't meant to serve
They have to love themselves
Have a positive self image
Love their independence
Don't feed them unimportant things
Like designer labels
Perfect faces and hair
To count calories
Teach them to value their lives
To see their importance in the world
Not according to other people
But as an individual
Without that the fairy tales
They read won't come true
How can they commit to someone
When they can't commit to themselves

Amy L. Phillips

Please

Allow me to forgive myself
For letting my heart break again

Relationship Blooms

Time stops, but only briefly to the world
To me, all is motionless
Erase my past ideals to draw a new humanity
You bring forth great pleasure to my soul
Wrap me tight with your love to drive out my fears
What angel from God sent you to me
The strength of your personality brings my own to flourish
But why do you push me away
I think you are afraid to love
Love makes you sturdy not weak
Your past prevents you from letting go
From running wild
Please don't be afraid to love me
Let our souls unite as one
To grow together in a perfect garden of roses and tulips
We can play games behind the lilacs
And give chase around the pond

Dear God, do give me the strength to continue my quest
Allow him to see inside himself
To a place never before reached
And let me fill it with baskets of petals

Please my dear, let me love you
Let me be your strength and you be mine
We shall travel through the gardens together

Amy L. Phillips

Please my dear meet me by the daffodils

Daddy's Pride

Summer came and away we went
To spend our weeks in fields
It wasn't much to me then
Just fields
But when he walked onto those fields
He saw the days of yore
He saw them marching
Spilling the blood of families
He felt their pain and triumphs
Their glory pierced through him
We sat along the path waiting
Wishing we were somewhere else
But this was important to him
He admired them
And what they did for our country
He was proud of his relation
Until now, it was just a field to me

The Day He Strayed

One day he came home late
With a different scent
I lay asleep on the couch
And awake to the opening door
Our eyes meet
He sits by my side
She, still asleep in bed did not come out
The air through the room was thick
We both knew without words
He would soon be gone
For what she thought, I did not know
He was different now
It was different now
Questions and answers were flying
Soon he was gone
I sat as though at the movies
Viewing from afar
The fruit had spoiled
Our lives to change forever
One will turn to three
Each taking separate paths
Love still as one

Father Left Me Twice

Unchained emotions freed him, ruined him
Stressful evil consumed him
And he moved
Both reach but continue to miss
Days become weeks
Weeks to months

One day he takes him from me too soon
Lives unfinished
An ending of two
Disassembled into one alone
Remember the will, the good

You gave me strength
You gave me disposition
Someday we shall walk again
Hand in hand
Until then we go on
We continue to grow

For you are always with me
Forever your princess
And I am not afraid to travel alone in body

To Dana

Through all of the hard times
You have been my crutch
Always there to help
No matter what time
To listen to tears
Comfort me in kindness
I can trust you with my life
For you have already saved me
Many times
A friendship I deeply treasure
Never selfish or judging
Just there
Needed like the air I breath

Missing You

Sometimes I reach for the phone to call you
And then I remember
Sometimes I need to ask your advice
And then I remember
Sometimes I need your guidance
And then I remember

I wonder why you had to go
Had to leave me so soon
My own selfishness tells me that I need you
I know you are at peace
I know that you are free

Your pain and suffering is over now
I know I will see you again
In another time, in another place

Please carry me through the hardships
And draw me to my conscious
Watch over me with a cautious eye
You are still my protector

Goodbye Father

I look back on all of the fun, on all of the countless memories
And I know why life is good
I know why I love you
I know what kind of person you shaped me into
A strong, caring, secure one
I know the importance of every day
Of every waking hour
I cherish the time I spent to you
I cherish every time I heard your voice
Every time you said you loved me
You showed me the boundless capacity of the human heart
And the powerful will of the human spirit
And I am always with you no matter how far away I may seem
And you are always with me no matter how far away you may seem
You impacted many people with your notable attitude and marvelous
wit
You are the best father anyone could have asked for
And for that, my love, respect, and admiration is eternal

The Ring

The 12th of September 1998
The day part of my heart left for heaven
To walk with you in the glorious wonder
And I shall carry your ring
The ring of your eternal union
The union of your true love
And when my true love is found
I too shall wear your ring
Reflecting your union in my own
And every day I look down at my hand
And every time I look at my true love
I shall remember you
So know, you are not forgotten
But rather a living testament in my life
To be with me forever
And some day, I shall meet you again
And then my heart will again be whole

Amy L. Phillips

Alone

Loneliness consumes my every part
And there I sit alone
There I dream alone
I see you far away
Enclosed in a jar
Taunting me with an eye
Pull close, but pushed away
Never to leave my heart
Fears are real, and alone I wait

Cage

My solitude has begun to encompass my all
Days are endless and nights are short
Deserts replace rivers once frequent
Deserts of soldiers
Driven forward by some unknown power
For fear their secret will be known
With loaded weapons they face battle
She looks in the glass
But her image is lost
Experiences become spats of sanity
Coupled with visions of freedom
The deep end is above my head
Yet I tread with dignity

Endless

Today is a day of entrapment
A day when a person turns into a white mouse
And is forced to run in a wheel
Never to have the scenery change
Never to feel a change in thoughts
You catch yourself looking around
Yet all you see is the same

Fear

How strange when fear leaves
The spider that once kept you at bay
Is now a speck on the wall
The noises in the night
No longer mischievous spirits – but wind
It's funny when you age
How your views remodel
How simple it was to be a child
To know only happy and sad
Love and hate
And Fear

Awaiting Therapy

I sit here among the people
Each doing their own
Trying to keep themselves occupied
All awaiting their name to be next

He walks to sit down
To find his safe place
Looking at a chair for two
But sits in the chair for one
His hesitation is evident

From his chair he looks up
But only briefly – for he is reading
To secretly see each passer by
Partly out of curiosity
Wondering why they are here
And if they can tell why he is here
His foot shakes with nervous quivers
What side of his mind will they explore today

She sits next to me with a gold sweater
Her scent is stale perfume
Her loneliness is silently visible
Absorbing the chair
And I feel pity for her

Two people, a couple, sit together
A younger woman, and an older man
Conversing as if no one else is around
Discussing how to remove a curse
She is relatively inexperienced - poor girl
He is a well-traveled, knowledgeable man
Constantly explaining to her
And then I go to the end of the hallway
And she walks too slowly
The door closes behind us
And I absorb into the chair in a secure cuddle
Remembering the stale perfume

Panic

So I don't like to be outside
I don't like to be around
Not all the time
Why do I hate for them to see me
I get so afraid
My mind runs wild
Don't pressure me into panic
It will come on its own
Trying to break me
Please God, save my mind

Dreams

I always find myself looking for things in my dreams
Be it something I lost
Or something I just can't seem to find
What does my mind constantly search for
Why do these scenes play over and over
A memory of peace
Searching for things I once had

In a house with lots of people I do not know
I sit on the ground
And out of the dirt she comes
And then I remember, she is dead
The rain comes down in mud flakes
It is also raining inside

The leaves are turning red, brown, yellow, and gold
The wind picks up from the east
A single leaf spun off the tree
It twirled, tipped, and toppled
Slowly it hit the ground
Gently cushioned by the tall green grass

I keep pulling the wrong levers
Outside is full of snow
Houses are overgrown with dead, brown, broken vines

Insomnia

By the light of one small flame I work
Unable to catch my dreams
My body over run with fatigue
Yet my mind drills me
Images of people and situations
A melody following closely behind
I close my eyes and try to remain still
Thinking perhaps I can fool myself
Minutes on the clock are racing
And I realize how much I will need them come morning
How my eyes will ache when the sun pours in
Soon I am overcome
And drift away
Only to rise more weary than the eve before
A night wasted
And I am left to try again
Never to break my routine

Fear of Sunlight

Your delusions make you who you are
And create their own mischief
To rule you by panic
Keeping you locked inside
Always one step behind yourself
Never to fully catch up to your mind
Constantly going in circles
And running through a maze
Terrified with every passing minute
Your haven is not around you
No safe, secure surroundings
Being constantly stricken by hysteria
A frenzied deranged circus in your brain
Clouds of twisters lingering above
To be human is to be flawed
And we strive toward good
Yet lend ourselves to evil
Our own free will shall be our demise
And our sanity forever marked
With the cruel compositions that lay before us

A Good Day

Today I am pleased
At full ease with my being
And everything if fresh

A Thin Line

How can I explain to you how much pain I feel on a daily basis
It amazes me how much my mind can change
How drama envelops my life
And why am I always so tired
Why is my body so exhausted
At times I like to be alone
I relish in my solitude
Free to do whatever I feel is needed at the time
To rely only upon myself
Not being forced to keep a specific schedule
Nor adhere to a fixed set of rules
No boundaries to keep within
But perhaps that is what I need the most
To keep my mind at ease
And to bring me back to the life I am use to
But then again, perhaps it is time to grow
And his newfound freedom is a way to force me
A way to force me to explore myself
But why is it so painful to dive into yourself
And why does it make you feel so alone
Like you are so different from the majority
I think this point of self-exploration is what sends fear
This is why most people turn away and follow crowds
This is the point that can drive a person insane
One false move will send you down
Past the depths of your soul

Amy L. Phillips

And into the realm of insanity

Today

Dollar bills run the family
Lies flow easily from our lips
Drugs more common than respect
Background searches on babysitters
Children tortured with divorce
Scandals no longer surprise
Murder no longer shocks
Family time overtaken by tv, computers, and cell phones
Internet porn free for 30 day trial
Values have disintegrated through the generations
Every child grows more defiant
Immediate gratification rules all
Drinking, drugs, sex
No one can tell us what to do
War on the horizon
Overcrowding in prisons
Abuse run rampant
Violence in education
Stolen welfare checks
Destruction for entertainment
Fast cash wins over hard work
Nations of hate
Twelve year olds becoming mothers
Murderous viruses spread through ignorance
Escaping responsibility via ecstasy
Cowards hide behind guns

Amy L. Phillips

Malpractice insurance more expensive than heart surgery
Elderly left to die in old age homes
Neglected children in every town
Using credit cards to pay for credit cards
Popping Xanax like popcorn

Waiting

Once again I find myself waiting
What seems to be an endless cycle in my life
Yet it does lend to patience
Something of which I never had much of
Also for reflection time
To review my experiences
And develop my expectations
It allows me to focus on the world
To stop while the rest hustles
To try not to let it pass me by
And to see the importance of every day
To learn how to value my time on earth
So when my day comes I feel no regret
Regret of things I could have done
And where I should have placed my energies
To know I lived the fullest
And have passed my earthly tests
So never again shall I fear waiting
Nor loose my lust for patience

Upstairs Neighbors

Noisy, drunk upstairs neighbors
Arguing over how difficult the GED test is
Work all week
To buy a six pack and a dime bag
Tripping over their own heavy feet
Drunk lady with no teeth is visiting
Greasy, bleached hair
Over permed
Vocabulary of a thirteen year old
Screaming at their children
Then leaving them alone for hours
Teaching them how to be failures too
Not intelligent enough to be ashamed
To be embarrassed of me hearing
To know their life is a wasted ruin

Black

I have come to embark on a journey of paranoia
Of constant shakes and nerves
To not be able to be even draw a straight line
My pen moves on its own

Selfish

Today I am being tried with the utmost pain
I cannot understand why I am forced to be alone
Even when I should have someone here
I remain alone
Left to think about all that surrounds me
And of what steps I must take to make my perfection
Perhaps I am a selfish person
Or at least have selfish qualities about me
Yet don't we all have these distractions
Aren't they always left to flourish in our minds
So we do expect the best for ourselves
And the same for those we love
So it is so wrong to have those feelings

Broken Wall

Sometimes I sit here and wonder why
Why I stay so pushed away
Feeling like I just can't get ahead
Unable to relieve my stress
Like my everything has been torn from me
My home, my happiness
I have seen death and felt human sorrow
I have come face to face with loss
Tragedy is my constant companion
Accompanied with my own meandering thoughts
And I am a survivor

Don't Look

Your imagination fades
Children are the truth
They are the colors of our lives
Sometimes I feel trapped
Trapped in my own house
Trapped in my own life

Waiting for Death

My realizations are far from accurate
As I sit her alone waiting for death
You cannot convince me any longer
And I feel my loyalties are in vain
So why try to see this through
My full circle has come
Faster than I had hoped
And the circle itself is smaller that I thought
Dimensions I had perceived
Now unable to fill a drop of rain
And when shall this all end
Forever bound I sit and ponder this
As I sit her alone waiting for death

Dead Room, Dead House

I have grown so tired of being alone
Even when people are about
I am still alone
And I try to keep company
Even though it isn't wanted
Perhaps I am forever to be alone
Without the comforts
Known to those who dare to love
So here I remain
Alone in this dead house
Cold on a summer's day
Placed outside of myself
Perhaps to ease
You don't bring me solace
That is why I keep you near
Knowing when you are next to me
My loneliness will never subside
So close to me you will stay
Until I can no longer take this life

Death Comes Quickly

My death comes quickly now
As I dive into my own existence
Where I can't be alone any longer
The last stitch on my tapestry
To go unfinished
Slowly unraveling as I am forgotten

Gardens no longer sprout from my being
But feed off my last inspiration
And I begin to chill from these thoughts
Contradicting myself with every breath

And do you ever think of me
The way I wish
The way I need you to
I have now come to terms
With my own reality
And I see through new eyes
And I realize
That my death comes quickly now

Rain

Today is a day to stay asleep
The sun is hidden
By bursting clouds of gray
Light patter of rain
Against the window
It massages me back to sleep
Again I awake
My body feels so heavy
Eyes can't adjust to the room
My pillow feels so soft
It is cold outside of the blankets
Making me snuggle in deeper

Number Four

Do everything in fours
Turn the light on four times
Check the alarm clock four times
Pull up my socks four times each foot
TV turned off only on channel four
Read four books a week
Open and close the microwave four times
Hang up the phone four times
Straighten the picture four times
Everything has its place
Nothing can be out of place
Don't give me three or five of anything
Only four
I must do things the same way
Every time
If a mistake is made
I must start over at the beginning

See

And I am right back where I always seem to be
A thoughtless daze
Alone in my own world facing things
With hazardous vision
So afraid of what will become
And at some point we have to relieve ourselves
And stop playing these games
Unaware of our surroundings
To creep freely
And I don't understand why life makes such turns
And chases us with our hands tied
And our eyes blindfolded
A strange sense
And how can one be so undesired
So cautious with every move
Afraid of what will be started
But equally afraid
Of what will not be started

Yarn

I stare at my own reflection
And see countless imperfections
Flaws so numerous
It's a wonder they don't become one
And engulf the surroundings
Creating that one natural flaw
How it all remains together is far beyond me

Locked In

Things are on a downward spiral
Excitement is all but gone
Perhaps my own desolation
Separates me from all accounts
From all actions
Alone I sit in this bareness
Captive by time

End

Mom,
My life is one continual, unforgiving circle after another.
I don't mean that you lead me to this by any means.
So don't believe you have for a second.
Everyone has their time when the end must come.
And I know that mine is at hand.
I love you and fully appreciate all the love and support you
have given me through the years.
I keep trying to pick myself up but it doesn't seem to come
together as I had hoped.
Please don't be disappointed in me but I feel I have no other
option and this will end all of my problems.
I love you with all of my heart and soul and couldn't have
asked for a better mother.
Soon I will be with you again.
All my love.
Amy.

Mr. Elephant & Mr. Rooster

Mr. Elephant, the jester, looks down on me
From the perch on which he sits
His smile is hauntingly familiar
Eyes glaring with knowledge of beyond
I know you come alive whilst I sleep
Injecting me with demons
To tickle me with anxiety
The magic you use is darker than black
A very satisfying experience
Your friend, Mr. Rooster is by your side
His screams make me submissive
The ancient qualities are buried deep within
You make him adjust my spine with his wings
Move my vertebrae one by one
Inserting chips to keep me found
I awake with no knowledge but pain
Feeling you and him dance away from my bed

Good Morning Prozac

Every morning I awake
Turn on the coffee pot
And take my medicine
Two little pills every day
It lets me feel like every one else
I get to look forward to every day

I still can cry and feel pain
But it doesn't steal all of my time
I don't fall into the deep pit
Like I use to
I can take a tissue to dry my tears
And go on with life
Just a good sleep
To awake to a better morning

I don't have to do all those crazed rituals
If I mess up
I don't have to start over
Everyone messes up sometimes
And it's ok that I do too

I don't have to panic about being
Alone when I am sad
Afraid that I will do something
To myself

I finally feel safe and secure
With myself
I am no longer scared to be alone

About the Author

Amy L. Phillips was born in Racine, Wisconsin and grew up in De Pere, Wisconsin. She currently resides in Hollister, Missouri with her four cats and a dog.